The Agan Chronicles

Barbara Paulding

Published by Happy Jack Publishing, LLC

Copyright © June 2015
By Barbara Paulding

All photographs and images used in this publication are family photos or purchased stock photos.

ISBN-10:0692468919
ISBN-13:9780692468913

DEDICATION

This book is dedicated to my grandfather, George Agan. Grandpa never heard of Earth Day, but as a farmer his main focus was on nurturing and protecting the land. He was an old fashioned farmer. When weeds appeared in his fields he didn't kill them with harsh, earth poisoning chemicals. He got out the cultivator, got rid of the weeds, and aerated the soil. He persevered.

ACKNOWLEDGMENTS

A special thanks to Happy Jack Publishing and my editor, Beth Burgmeyer. Once again she has taken a rough manuscript and turned it into something I'm proud of. I am very grateful for her expertise and help.

AUTHOR'S NOTE

This is s book of memories. The memories are mine. Others may have different memories of these people and events. If my memories are faulty, the mistakes are mine and mine alone. As Charles Frazier points out in his novel, *Thirteen Moons*, memories are very unreliable. "After they've passed, events are only as your memory makes them, and they shift shape over time."

PROLOGUE

The Agan Chronicles is a book of memories, memories of my mother's families: the Agans and the Croys. As I look back on the Agan and Croy families, the central core of their lives seemed to be a longing for, and love of, the land.

In these families, farms were cherished, farms were lost, and when families were forced to live without land they felt displaced. This longing for land, for forty, eighty, a hundred acres, was a constant ache.

The story of my mother's family is one of hard times and poverty, triumph and tragedy. It is a story of dreams deferred, and always, this longing for the land.

Southern Iowa Farm

THE BEGINNING

Thelma Ethyl Agan was born on February 6, 1912, somewhere in Marion County Iowa. At the time of her birth her father, George, was working as a hired hand on one of the larger farms in the county. Her mother, twenty-three-year old Edna, was a farm wife who had given birth two years earlier to a son, John.

Iowa winters were frequently bitter, challenging times, but the winter of 1912 was the worst one in thirty-two years. It was so cold that year that when men went out to measure the depth of the ice on the Mississippi River they were amazed to find that it was 24-32 inches thick.

During that terrible winter Thelma was born at home in the drafty, cold house that the farmer provided for his hired man. There was no electricity, no running water, and no central source of heat. The kitchen cook stove and the potbellied coal stove, which stood in the main room, were the only sources of heat. Both stoves had to be "stoked" constantly to insure that they didn't go out. In the first few weeks after Thelma's birth it must have taken almost all of Edna's strength just to keep the fires going so her babies wouldn't freeze.

I have often wondered what George and Edna thought of their new little baby girl. Everyone in their family had dark hair and dark skin. They must have been surprised to see this new person, a tiny girl with beautiful red hair and porcelain skin. Edna seemed to cherish her little daughter's appearance. When Thelma was about six months old Edna carefully cut a curl from Thelma's hair, tied it with a green ribbon, and pressed it in one of the few books her family owned.

Somehow they all survived the winter, and with the advent of spring, things became a little easier for the family. News from the wider world began to make its way from the small towns to the farms of rural Iowa. In April they heard about the loss of the Titanic, the majestic ocean liner that was supposed to be unsinkable.

The Titanic

Some man named Henry Ford was building a car called the Model T, "a car for the masses." George just laughed when he heard that, and said, "If you have a hard time putting food on the table how can you afford a damn car?"

Model T Car

That November the nation went to the polls to elect their next president. There were three candidates that year: the current republican president, William Howard Taft, the democratic candidate, Woodrow Wilson, and former president Teddy Roosevelt, the Bull Moose candidate. George voted, as he always did, for the democratic candidate, Woodrow Wilson. Wilson was elected and the nation waited to see if things would improve under his leadership.

Of course when your family is struggling just to survive, sometimes the events of the outside world do not seem very important to you. George and Edna had to work hard to make sure their babies had enough to eat, and that they had enough wood and coal set aside for the next inevitable winter.

MY MOTHER'S FATHER: GEORGE AGAN

George was born in 1886 in Marion County near the little town of Gosport, Iowa. His father, Lewis Agan, and his mother, Mary Nancy Williamson Agan, were farmers. They lived on the eighty acre farm Lewis had inherited from his father. The family farm sat on a high hill called Agan Ridge. It was given this name because George's grandfather had given each of his six sons eighty acres along the ridge.

Road Leading up to Agan Ridge

George had two older sisters, Nancy and Kathleen (Kate), and an older brother John. After George was born the family continued to grow. He had a younger sister, Elsie, who died when she was thirteen, the twins Earl and Clarice Pearl, and his youngest brother, Stephen (Pete). Clarice Pearl died in infancy.

George started working on his father's farm almost as soon as he could walk. They raised pigs, cows, chickens and ducks. Milking cows, slopping hogs, gathering eggs, and planting and harvesting crops kept all of the children busy. George developed the farmers' habit of rising early in the morning. Even when George was in his sixties, when there were no cows to milk or pigs to feed, he still got up before five every morning.

George and his brothers and sisters all went to school in Gosport, a small, country school which went through the eighth grade. At that time an eighth grade education was considered sufficient for most young people.

When George grew up he only wanted one thing: to be a farmer. Unfortunately at that time, the oldest son always inherited the family farm, so Lewis left the farm to George's older brother, John. George had to try to find another way to make a living. After he married and had a family he tried many different kinds of work. He worked as a hired hand, a miner, and a salesman for Raleigh Products. When he was forced to work in the mines he and his family moved from coal mining town to coal mining town.

Main Street in Melcher

Southern Iowa Coal Mine

He took his family to Lawrence, Kansas, Colorado Springs, Colorado and Richland, California, all in an attempt to make enough money to get back to the land, to get home to Marion County.

It must have been hard for him, not having his own land, having to work for other successful farmers. He was a proud man and it must have pained him to see his family living in poverty.

Once when my mother was eight, a neighbor accused George of breaking into his smokehouse and stealing some meat. When the sheriff came to question George, he found a lot of fresh meat in the house. The sheriff arrested George and took him and the meat away, leaving his wife, Edna, with some very frightened and hungry children.

George, who was thirty-four at the time, insisted that he was innocent, but no one believed him. There was a trial and George's sister-in-law, Pearl Klootwyk, testified on his behalf. She swore that she and her husband Harmon had just butchered their hogs and had given one to George to help his family. My mom said she never knew if Pearl really gave them the meat or if her dad had stolen it. She believed he would have stolen it, if that had been the only way to keep his children fed. If Pearl lied under oath, it was a very brave thing for that little religious woman to do.

No matter what George did there was never enough money to get the farm he longed for. Times were desperate and the depression made everything harder. One summer two of George's son's, Buster and Don, went to Colorado Springs to try to get work. They had heard that the army was hiring men to help build Fort Carson. They wrote back and told George there was a lot of work available. So George and my dad, Jim, decided to go. They were planning to ride freight trains all the way to Colorado Springs but they were not very successful railroad bums. They hopped a freight in Albia but were picked up at the next stop in Chariton, just twenty five miles down the line. They spent the night in jail. The next morning the sheriff took all of Dad's money and bought them both bus tickets as far as their money would take them. Unfortunately, that was only as far as Ogallala, Nebraska. They were picked up in Ogallala for vagrancy and spent another night in jail.

The next day they started walking and hitching, trying to get to Colorado Springs. When they got to Colorado Springs, George's feet were bloody from so much walking. They went out to the gates of Fort Carson and waited for Don and Buster to come out. The next day they applied for jobs and were hired immediately. They soon had enough money to send for my immediate family, my grandma Edna, and my aunt, Dana. My grandmother Edna fried chicken and made a batch of sugar cookies so we would all have plenty to eat on the train. My older brother, Jimmy, and I bounced from one side of the train to the other, trying to be the first one to see the mountains.

Jim, Thelma, and Barbara Paulding at the train station in Colorado Springs

We had a wonderful summer in Colorado.

Thelma, Barbara, and Jimmy Paulding: Garden of the Gods, Colorado Springs

When summer ended we returned to Pershing, Iowa but after a short time George took his family to Lawrence, Kansas, looking for work, always trying to find the job that would enable them to buy that Iowa farm.

That dream remained out of reach until the Second World War. When the United States entered the war, the Government started building ships. So George moved his family to California to work in the shipyards. With George and two of his sons working in the shipyards it seemed that the dream of having their own farm would finally come true. They lived together in an apartment, the wages were good, and they all gave their paychecks to Edna to keep safe for them.

The Last Liberty Ship Ever Built

When they came back from California three years later, they came to our house in Deep River. We were all sitting around the big dining room table, eating supper, when George asked Edna to get the money.

Left to Right: Buster Agan, Edna Agan, Bob Agan (standing), George Agan, Jim Paulding, Tommy Paulding, Thelma Agan Paulding, Barb Paulding, Phyllis Agan

He wanted to see how much they had saved for a farm. Edna got up, brought her purse to the table, and handed the money bag to George. When he pulled out the money he looked sick. There was only $800 in the bag. "Where's the money, Edna," he asked quietly.

Edna looked scared but her voice was defiant. "It's in California. I spent it. Playing bingo. I won at first, then I started losing. I tried to win it back…"

George slammed his fist on the table. "You lost thousands and thousands of dollars, all that work, the savings!" George pushed his chair back and went out the back door. It was the only time anyone ever remembered seeing George lose his temper.

I was totally confused by everything that had happened. I had played Bingo at the little county fairs where the games only cost a dime. How could my Grandma have lost thousands of dollars playing Bingo? Dad explained that there was something called high stakes Bingo, which cost hundreds of dollars to play. You could win a lot but you could also lose a lot. My grandma lost a lot.

Even though most of the money was gone, George was still able to buy an eighty acre farm on Cedar Creek, near Marysville, Iowa. It was a hardscrabble farm that had been strip mined and ill-used. There was some bottom land, and when it didn't flood, the crops from that piece of land were good. There was also plenty of pasture for the cows and horses. Even though it was rough, and not too productive, it was still a farm. It was his own place.

Hillside at Cedar Creek Farm

The farmhouse was a big white clapboard building which sat at the top of a long hill. A hilly, rutted dirt road led up to the house. There was a nice big red barn which sat at the top of another long hill. I remember the hay mow and the stanchions for the milk cows. There were also several smaller outbuildings that were used for hogs, chickens, tools, etc. There was no water in the house. The only working well was at the bottom of the long hill. There was a cistern that Edna could use for washing and baths, but the drinking water had to be carried up the hill. With no water source there was no indoor plumbing, so the outhouse, which stood across the lane from the house, was a necessity. When they first moved to the farm there was no electricity. I loved being there in the evenings, loved how the soft light from the kerosene lamps cast friendly shadows on the faces I loved.

George had a small herd of milk cows and he also raised hogs and chickens, ducks and geese. He had a team of work horses: Babe and Brownie. Somehow he made enough money to live on. Two of his sons, Buster and Don, lived on the farm with them. Sometimes the boys would mine some of the land, sinking shallow tunnels into the hills and chipping out the coal. They used some of the coal to heat their house and sold some on the open market.

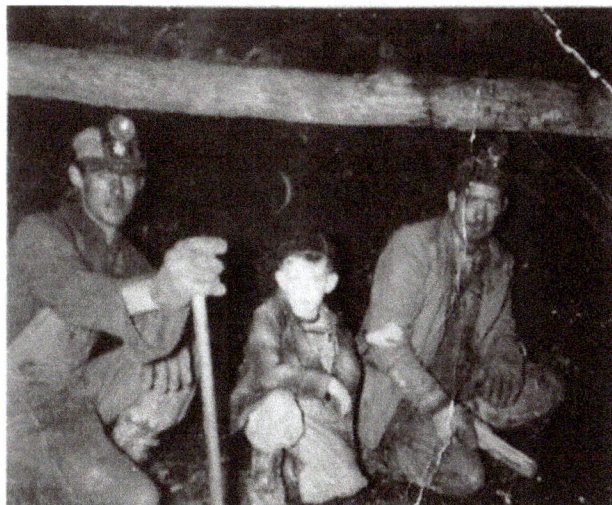

Left to Right: Don Agan, Tommy Paulding, Buster Agan

George loved living on that farm, even though it was a hard life. He was a good farmer and was somehow able to eak out a living on those eighty acres. They had some good years when the floods didn't come and the hog market was good. I can remember my whole family being in the fields, helping George husk the corn. I loved doing that, loved riding back up the hill in the wagons filled with corn.

I don't know what kind of a father George was. He was a quiet man. Maybe he seemed distant to his children, but I do know he loved them. He was close to my Dad and told him how it hurt him when he saw any of his sons drunk. He was proud of his children's accomplishments and happy when his daughters became teachers.

I do know what kind of a Grandpa he was. He was quiet, reserved and he gave us all a great gift: the gift of his time.

He taught me how to feed a baby calf out of a bucket, how to milk a cow, and how to run the corn planter that he pulled behind his old Ford tractor. He took me to my first livestock auction and told me not to scratch my nose or we might end up buying a cow we didn't want. He always took the time to let my brother Tommy and I ride Babe, the old grey work horse. Grandpa would put the bridle on Babe and then help us up. There was no saddle so we learned to ride bareback. I think he was really crazy about Tommy, loved to listen to his chatter.

Jim Paulding and Tommy Paulding riding Babe

On hot summer days we often begged to go swimming in the creek. Grandpa usually put aside what he was doing and took us down to Cedar creek where he sat under a tree, watching over us. When we got back to the farm house Mom sometimes said, "Boy he never did that for us when we were growing up."

Old Swimming Hole at Cedar Creek

It seems like every weekend everyone came to my Grandparents' farm: John and Dorothy, Pearl and Harmon, sometimes Grace and Walter. One by one the families would start to leave. After each departure George would always say, "Well, we finally got rid of them." Once I asked him if he said that after we left. He grinned and said, "No, of course not, Barbara."

Sometimes I wondered how they managed to feed all of their weekend visitors. Buster usually killed a couple of chickens, dunked them in hot water, pulled out their feathers and singed off the pin feathers with a burning newspaper. Grandma dressed the chickens and fried them up. She was an awesome cook. If it was summer, we usually made ice cream in the evening, using the cream from Grandpa's cows.

In all the time I knew him, he was tall and straight with coal black hair. But after his son, Don, died, George's hair seemed to turn grey overnight.

George Agan and His Son, Don Agan

He died shortly after that in the Oakdale Sanatorium. The doctors initially thought that he had TB but it turned out to be lung cancer. Even those short stints in the mines had been enough for him to develop black lung disease. We all went to the hospital many times to see him. I was fourteen years old and when I was finally allowed to go in and see him I just held onto his hand. He looked at me and said, "I don't think I'm going to beat this one, Barbara." I couldn't lie to him so I didn't say anything except, "I love you Grandpa."

I have a clear picture in my head of who my grandpa was. He rolled his own cigarettes and listened to the news everyday on the radio. He admired and respected Franklin Roosevelt and never missed his fireside chats. When the president was talking you knew you had to be very quiet. He voted Democratic, never went to church and finally realized his dream of having a farm. When he worked in the mines he joined the union but he was not a union man or a miner. He was a farmer. He persevered.

MY GRANDPA

By Barbara Paulding

The little calf is almost as big as me.
Hungry
Smelling sweetly of milk
You give me a pail
Tell me to feed the little critter

I try
The calf butts the bucket, spilling half of the milk
Stands there bawling
I am close to tears

"Damn it Barbara"

You stop then.
"Here try this"
You dip my fingers in the milk. Place them in the calf's mouth.

The calf sucks
Greedily
I lower my fingers into the bucket
The calf sucks up the milk

You smile at me
"Now that's how you teach a calf to drink out of a bucket"

I smile up at you
Feel sweet and clean inside

MY MOM'S MOTHER: EDNA NORA CROY

Edna was born in 1889 on her father, Martin Croy's farm in Marion County Iowa. Martin and his wife, Lucinda, owned a thousand acres near Gosport, Iowa.

Edna had one older brother, Ansel, four younger brothers, Homer, Bryan, Clarence and Glenn, and two younger sisters, Grace and Pearl. Martin was a very successful farmer. He had a large herd of cattle, and raised hogs, corn, oats and hay. Martin farmed the land with work horses. Sometimes Martin shipped his cattle to the Chicago Stockyards to sell them. He always went to Chicago with his cattle. If he got a good price he brought presents back for his wife and children. One year he brought his wife Lucinda a beautiful tea set. That tea set is still in the family.

Tea Set

So Edna grew up in a very prosperous farm family. She worked hard, as all farm children did, but her family never wanted for anything. Edna learned to do all of the things expected of a young girl in those days. She learned how to can food, dress chickens, help when the family butchered a hog, run the separator, churn butter, and of course she helped with the cooking, cleaning, laundry and sewing.

All of the Croy children attended the little country school at Gosport.

Gosport School Today

Things were very good for the Croy family until Martin died in 1918. Edna was married to George by then, but she had to watch as her family farm was gambled away by her brothers. As was customary at that time, Ansel, the oldest son inherited the farm. Ansel started spending money recklessly, bought a big fancy riding horse, hired most of the farm work done, and gambled. He bought a small house for his mother, Lucinda, and moved her to Melcher Dallas.

George kept telling Edna, "You girls better do something or that whole farm is going to be gone." Edna did talk about it with her sisters, Grace and Pearl, but they could never figure out what they could do. So the thousand acre farm was sold to pay gambling debts. It must have been hard for Edna to watch her family's home disappear.

As a young mother, dealing with bone crushing poverty, having a new baby every two years, and having no home to call her own, Edna seemed to have lost her way. She frequently neglected many of her basic responsibilities: cooking, cleaning, and caring for her small children. There are conversations that still haunt my memories. My aunts and uncles told me that my mother, Thelma, had to take over these tasks at a very early age. They talked about not having enough to eat and how things really fell apart when my mother left home to go to high school. There were conversations about Edna smoking and drinking at a time when "proper women" did neither. Conversations, and yet…there were post cards from those early days, written from Edna to her sister, Pearl, post cards about the children and everyday happenings. Letters from a woman who did love her children, who worried when they were sick. Those postcards gave no hint of a woman suffering from any debilitating depression. And yet, things were not right. Things were undeniably very difficult for Edna, George and all of the children.

I have a difficult time reconciling the grandma Edna I knew and the Edna of those early, hard years before she had grandchildren. Who was the Edna that I grew up with, the grandmother I knew and loved?

Edna holding Barbara Paulding

Edna was a large woman with a pretty face and sweet smile. She liked people, was outgoing and friendly. Edna was a wonderful cook and loved to tell stories. After they bought their farm in 1946, Edna spent many hours fishing, sitting on the bank at Cedar Creek, neglecting housework and other chores. One day, Edna was at the house and my dad came up from the creek with a big catfish. When he put the fish in a large wash basin, it was so big it stretched end to end. Edna left the food on the stove, grabbed her fishing pole and headed for Cedar Creek. A half an hour later she was back with an even bigger catfish whose tail went halfway up the side of the basin.

When we went to Minnesota on our annual fishing trips, Edna always fished from the dock. She would not get in the boats. Still, she usually ended up catching more fish than the men. One year, we rented a cabin near Dead Lake. Everyone said there weren't any fish in there. Edna went down to the lake "just to check it out." She started pulling bullheads out one right after the other. So all of the family started fishing in Dead Lake. That was the year we took home three big barrels of salted, iced fish.

Edna Croy Agan

People liked her. As an adult I heard many stories of her kindness. An old family friend told me that she literally saved him from starving when he was a boy. He told me she fed him and gave him food to take home when his family had nothing. He used to go fishing with her when he was little and he laughed as he remembered how she used to climb through barbed wire fences to get to a good fishing spot.

Unfortunately, Edna was like her bother Ansel in her love of gambling. That's how she lost all of the men's wages in California, and lost the family's dream of a prosperous Iowa farm.

Edna was also something of a hypochondriac, always concerned that there was something wrong with her. Sometimes she would go from doctor to doctor insisting they find something wrong. She took a lot of pills as she got older. There were times when no other doctor would do except Doc Mater in Knoxville. Once, when she was living in Des Moines with her children, and no one had time to take her to Knoxville, she called a cab and went to see Doc Mater. That was an expensive doctor's visit!

I imagine that for most of her life Edna must have felt like a displaced person. She and George moved so often and only really had a home of their own once they bought the farm on Cedar Creek.

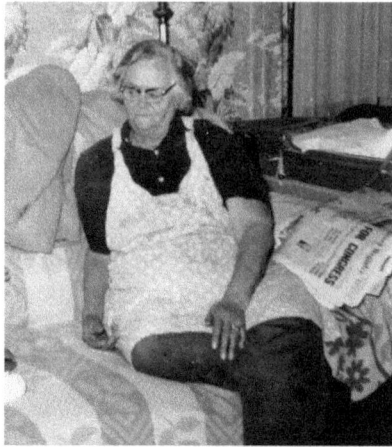

Edna at Cedar Creek Farm

Edna's youngest sister, Pearl, saved things including most of the post cards she received throughout her life. Of course Edna wrote to her many, many times. In the cards she received from Edna there were often instructions about where to send the mail the next time Pearl wrote.

OCTOBER 2, 1915

Dear Pearl, how are you all? We are all well, just got your letter today. Will send his (one of Edna's brothers) shoes as soon as I can. Don't send any more mail to Buxton. We are going to move tomorrow. You write right away and send the Boys (Edna's brothers) addresses again for I lost the letter before. Tell them both hello for me. When you write be sure and send their addresses for I want to write to them to send our mail to same address at Melrose as it was last time we moved. I will write as soon as we get moved from here.

NOVEMBER 21, 1916

Hello Pearl. How are you? I am going to come home about next Saturday if I can. Will write you a letter soon. Send my mail to Tipperary, Iowa.

After George died in 1951 Edna lived with her son, Buster, or her daughter, Dana. She had very little income, had never paid into social security, so she received an old age pension. She was dependent on the kindness of her children, a kindness that was always there. Whenever we went on a fishing trip we took her with us. Even when she was in her late sixties, she loved going and never complained about the long hours in the car.

I never knew the Grandma who smoked and drank. She quit all of that when my older brother Jimmy was born.

Don Agan, Edna Croy Agan, Jimmy & Barbara Paulding

She didn't want her grandchildren to think badly of her. She was a wonderful grandma to me. She had the warmest hugs, was never cross and was not fussy about her house. She taught me how to clean a chicken, how to use the separator, and make butter. Whenever we made butter she kept the buttermilk for pancakes and cookies. She also drank it. She loved buttermilk. She taught me many poems, stories and songs. I remember them all to this day.

Edna was a letter writer. She wrote me many letters when I was in college. I only kept one. Her notes were full of everyday happenings, a touch of home. I loved her very much.

OCTOBER 18, 1957

Dear Barbara will write you a few lines tonight, your daddy just brought me up home, I went down to stay with Tommy, he got wet at a football game Monday, has a terrific cold. hope it isn't that Asiatic flu.

...They have never heard a word from Jimmy, he told them he would call and has had plenty of time to get a letter back. I think he is okay but it makes one wonder.

...I should go to Knoxville to see Dr Mater but I don't know from one minute to the next what I can do, I called him this week he had not heard from Iowa City.

...Did you get to look for that book Castle in the Swamp hope you find it.

Lots of love gram & all

GEORGE AND EDNA'S MARRIAGE

George and Edna were two young people when they met, both from successful farming families. When they got married I'm sure they both had the expectation of living their lives on a farm somewhere, living the only kind of life they both knew.

But how does a young couple get a farm, when by an accident of birth, both of their family farms had gone to their brothers? George tried. He worked as a hired hand, as a coal miner and even tried being a salesman. With all of his effort and hard work, the family remained poor.

The stories my mother and her brothers and sisters told did not paint a picture of a happy home. Edna was very jealous of George and always accused him of seeing other women. Every night when he came home, bone tired and feeling defeated, she started in on him, accusing him of being unfaithful, complaining about being so poor, complaining and complaining and complaining. George didn't respond, never fought back, just lay down in bed and tried to get some sleep. Sometimes she was still yelling at him when he climbed out of bed to get ready for the next day's work. The children tried to block out the noise, to block out the sound of their mother's voice. It didn't work. They wondered how their dad could just lay there and listen to that night after night after night.

Long after his parents had died Buster told me about the summer he was eleven years old and went to work on a neighbor's farm. He was staying at the neighbor's house and had been away for six weeks when he got terribly homesick. He asked the farmer if he could go home for the night and come back to work the next afternoon. The farmer was a kind man and told Buster he could go and stay the whole day if he wanted to. Buster walked the three miles back to his house after he finished the day's chores. It was dark when he got home and as he approached the back door he heard his mother's strident voice rising and falling in bitterness. He didn't even open the door, just turned around and walked the three miles back to the neighbors, climbed in bed and listened to the blessed sounds of silence. Buster later told me, "I guess I had just forgotten how bad it was, Barbara."

George and Edna never divorced, but in later years they had separate bedrooms and that seemed to bring some peace to their relationship. Sometimes old age can help to heal things. I think that was the case for my grandparents. The passions and anger of younger years seemed to be gone. While they lived on the farm, when George got up at five every morning, Edna was always up with him, cooking him a big farmer's breakfast. When the relatives praised her cooking on their weekend visits, George would smile and say, "This is nothing. You should see the food she cooks when you're not here." That always brought a smile to Edna's face.

Tommy Paulding, Harmon Klootwyk, Connie, Don Agan

When George died, shortly after their son Don died, Edna was a woman in pain, a woman who had lost the man she loved.

MY MOM'S BROTHER: JOHN AGAN

John was my mother's older brother. He had black hair, brown eyes and dark skin. He was a smart little boy, and was a kind and loving big brother. One of the few stories my mother told about her early childhood was the story of John and the pitchfork. When my mother was about four she and John were out playing in the haymow when John threw a pitchfork and accidently hit my mother in the foot. He started sobbing and ran down the ladder wailing, "I hit Sissy with the pitchfork. I hit Sissy with the pitchfork." When Edna heard the ruckus and finally understood what John was saying she imagined the worst and hurried toward the barn. She was very relieved to find that my mother just had a small cut on her foot. She had to spend more time comforting John than she did fixing my mother's foot.

John was an excellent student and was especially good at math. He was on the track team at Knoxville and had the opportunity to travel around Iowa for track meets. After high school he worked at different jobs, but he usually came home on weekends. On one of these visits, when he was out cutting weeds for his dad, he cut his arm. It wasn't a bad cut, just a scratch really, so John kept working. A few days later, John was in trouble. The cut had become infected and he developed blood poisoning. In the days before antibiotics this was a life threatening situation. When the red line indicating infection kept getting higher and higher on his arm, the doctors told him they would have to amputate his arm to save his life.

I can't begin to imagine what this did to John's life. How did he handle going from a healthy, whole young man to losing an arm and living for the rest of his life with a metal hook? I think he was like his dad. He persevered.

Sometime after he recovered he married Dorothy Green from neighboring Bussey.

Dorothy and John Agan

John and Dorothy never had any children, but they did help to raise Dorothy's sister's girls, Vicky and Connie. When they brought the girls home, they were living on a small farm about a mile down the road from Grandpa's farm. I remember how excited I was when the girls came to live with John and Dorothy. Even though they were a few years younger than me, I was happy to have some cousins around when we went to the farm!

Vicky

Connie

Despite the loss of his arm, John was an able worker and was always successful at any job he held. He had no trouble driving a car, or other machinery, and was always able to provide for his family. He worked as a farmer, a coal miner and went to Detroit, Michigan to work for the Ford Motor Company. He retired from Ford with a good pension and also got a settlement for Black Lung Disease from his time working in the mines.

None of this seems to really adequately provide a window into John's life. He was a great card player and knew how to count cards, so he usually knew what was in his opponent's hand. He excelled at cribbage but he never carelessly gambled his money away.

Whenever he played poker with his brother, Buster, John invariably won. Buster would get frustrated, throw his cards down, and say, "What's the use of playing, you already know what I have in my hand."

He was a quiet man with a quiet sense of humor. He loved Vicky and Connie very much and really enjoyed being a grandpa to their children.

Dorothy & John: Anniversary Celebration

MY MOTHER'S BROTHER: MERRILL (BUSTER) AGAN

Buster seemed to break the mold for Agan men. Physically he ran true to form. He was tall, had dark hair, and a dark complexion. However, his personality and demeanor seemed to be closer to his mother, Edna. Buster was outgoing, laughed a lot and was very kind and easy going with his young nieces and nephews.

Buster Agan, Jimmy, Barbara & Jim Paulding

Whenever he came to our house he usually had a package of gum or a candy bar for us. One day he brought me a package of gum, and as I went around the room giving everyone a piece, I found I only had one piece left when I got to Buster. "You didn't want any did you, Buster?" I asked. Of course he said he didn't so I got the last piece of gum.

Once when my brother Jimmy and I got our childhood shots, Buster told us he would buy us an ice cream cone if we didn't cry. I worked really hard not to cry but Jimmy did cry when he got his shot. Our kind hearted uncle bought us both ice cream cones. I remember feeling a little bit cheated. I wondered why I had bothered to try so hard not to cry!

Buster was very loyal to his family and friends. When he was in tenth grade at Knoxville, his younger brother, Don, was accused of some wrong doing and suspended from school. Buster was sure Don was innocent and tried to get the principal to change his mind. He didn't, so Buster walked out and never returned to school. Don did return and graduated from high school in Hamilton.

Although he only had a tenth grade education, Buster always had good jobs. He worked on farms, in the mines, in the ship yards building liberty ships, on road crews, and for a Des Moines construction company called Cico Steel. Cico Steel laid floors for large commercial buildings all around the state of Iowa. Buster was soon promoted to foreman and was a master at reading the complicated blueprints. He was physically strong, personable and respected by his crew of workers.

Buster Agan & Coworker

Buster differed from his dad and his older brother when it came to drinking and gambling. Buster drank, and sometimes he drank a lot. He also gambled. He played poker, and later in life, loved betting on the horses. Buster won a lot, lost a lot, and sometimes got in terrible fights over poker games. One night, when I was ten, and Buster was staying with us in Deep River, he came home really late. I heard a lot of noise and came down stairs to see what was going on. Buster's shirt was bloody and my mom was trying to clean his wound, a wound he'd gotten in a knife fight after a poker game. I was really scared, but when he saw me standing in the door he just grinned at me and said, "I'll be all right, Bardie. You go on back to bed." Reassured, I went back to bed.

Buster never married. After his dad died, he lived with his mom on the Cedar Creek farm and took care of her for the rest of her life.

Buster and his nephew, Dan Agan at the Cedar Creek Farm

When his youngest sister, Dana, divorced her husband, and had small children to care for, Buster helped her. They eventually bought a house together in Pleasant Hill and he helped Dana raise her children.

He was a very important person in the lives of Dana's children, Debbie and Jeff. He loved them very much.

Jeff, Buster, and Debbie

There are many wonderful stories about Buster. When they all still lived on the Cedar Creek farm Buster, who was in his thirties, frequently drove the old green Chevy pickup into Bussey to spend some time in the bars. If we were there he would often take my brother, Tommy, and me with him. We went in the taverns and he set us up on the bar stools. Buster had a few beers and he always bought Tommy and me orange pop. When he drove back to the farm, after having a few beers, he always drove very slowly and very carefully. My parents never seemed to worry about us when we were with Buster.

Tommy's favorite Buster story happened when Tom was about eight years old. They went into a bar and Tommy was hungry so Buster ordered a hamburger for him. Buster drank his beer, Tommy drank his pop, but still no hamburger. When Buster asked the bartender about it, he made some snide remark and Buster got mad. He reached across the bar, grabbed the guy by the shirt and lifted him halfway across the bar. "Get the boy his hamburger and get it now." I guess it didn't take long after that for the hamburger to arrive.

Buster never stopped gambling. After he and Dana bought their house in Pleasant Hill, they drove to Omaha almost every weekend to the race track. For a long time he was a very successful gambler. He studied the horses, jockeys, and trainers and won quite a bit of money. His winning streak seemed to end one weekend when a pick pocket got away with his billfold which had about $6000.00 in it. Dana's son, Jeff, always said that winning didn't come as easily for Buster after that.

Buster taught me a very valuable lesson about gambling when he was on his winning streak. My husband and I were broke, and I asked Buster if he would take a twenty and bet it for me next weekend. "Can you afford to tear that twenty up and throw it out the window?" he asked.

I was horrified and said, "No, of course not."

Buster looked at me for a long time and then he said, "Then you can't afford to bet it." Those words of advice have stayed with me to this day.

Buster was such a giving man. Whenever he bought a new car he usually gave his old one to someone in the family, rather than trading it in. Around this same time, when I was out of work, he gave me his old Chevy. I drove that car for years.

Like his dad, he had a lot of favorite sayings. When it rained he usually said, "Do you think the rain will hurt the rhubarb?" or "This will make the pasture grow!"

He gave me two nick names when I was just a baby. He used to call me "Barbara Jean, Coffee Bean" and "Black Bardie Bambino." I could never figure out the latter one. Maybe it came from the fact that I was born in the Little Black House. As I got older he used to tell me, "Barbara, if you don't lose that smile you'll always be all right."

I often think that every child should have an uncle like Buster. He was a heroic figure in our young eyes. When we grew up, our adult eyes saw him, not as a heroic figure, but as a complete person, flawed but still wonderful, someone we cherished and loved.

Buster Agan

MY MOTHER'S BROTHER: DON AGAN

Don in Eighth Grade

Don was physically like his brothers, tall, dark, good looking. He was quiet like his dad, never drank, and was a very kind person. Don was not as outgoing as Buster but he seemed happy, smiled readily. Like his older brother, Buster, Don never married.

Don Agan's High School Graduation Picture

When World War II started Don tried to enlist in the army but he was rejected because he was totally deaf in one ear.

Don Agan (far right) Recruiting Picture

Instead he worked hard on the farm, in the mines, at Camp Carson, and in the shipyards of California. He was always there, part of the fabric of our family's life.

The Agans didn't seem to have much interest in music, but Don had a harmonica he cherished. He played a lot of the old tunes; one of his favorites was The Red River Valley. He could make his harmonica talk, playing long lonesome train whistles, and happy skipping tunes. Except for the songs my Grandma taught me, Don was the only person in the Agan family who made his own music.

After Grandpa bought the Cedar Creek farm, the entire Agan family returned to California to retrieve their belongings. They planned to take my older brother, Jimmy, with them. I was nine at the time and felt desolate. Not only were my favorite people in the world going away again, they were taking my brother with them and leaving me behind. I begged them to take me too, to no avail. They said I was too young

The morning they left I sobbed and sobbed, feeling like I would never stop crying. Don came over, sat with me, pulled his harmonica out of his pocket, and put it in my hands.

"Now you keep this safe for me. You practice, and when I get back, I want to hear you make that train whistle blow." I never did learn how to play the harmonica but I took special care of it. When they got back I returned it to Don, the man who could make it sing.

Don never married, and as far as I know he never dated anyone. He lived with his mom, dad, and brother, Buster. When we visited them on the farm he was always part of our all night card games, fishing and swimming days. He always went with us on our annual Minnesota trips.

Don loved trees and he planted many fruit trees on the hillside of the farm. Down the hill from the house, near the only working well on the place, he planted a big strawberry patch. That patch was carefully tended, and every June when the berries came in we picked them and had big bowls of strawberries covered with the cream from Grandpa's cows. I loved strawberries and cream. Sometimes Don would kid me and say if I didn't stop eating all those berries I would be as big as my Grandma. Since I was just a stick of a kid in those days, I just kept right on eating those strawberries.

Don at Cedar Creek Farm

I usually spent a week or two on the farm every summer. If Dana was home from her teaching jobs she would sometimes take me with her to the dances in Bussey. One night, when I was twelve, and we were at the dance it started to rain. The roads leading back to the farm quickly turned to mud, and we got stuck. Pretty soon Don came looking for us on the old tractor. He was soaked by the rain but just grinned at us, hooked up the chain and pulled us out. Dana told me later that night that Don had always been her favorite brother, that she loved how kind he was and was so proud of him for never drinking. She said he never fought and never caused any trouble.

The summer I turned fourteen something happened to Don. No one in the family knew what was wrong but Dana's favorite brother was gone. In his place was a tortured stranger. Like most of the Agans, Don was not religious but that summer he began reading the Bible every night, asking my brother Jimmy and I questions about some of the things he read. He started drinking heavily, and almost every night he got in the old green Chevy truck and drove around the back roads, honking the horn, endlessly. Sometimes he didn't even drive the truck, just sat in the driveway and honked the horn. The summer evenings that used to be filled with laughter, card games, and homemade ice cream now seemed like some torturous imitation of our former lives.

Nobody knew what was wrong with Don and nobody knew what to do. I overheard the adults speaking in worried tones, but they did nothing. This was long before people knew very much about mental illness, or knew there was help for it. Of course people tried to help. Sometimes when Don was in the truck blowing the horn, Buster would go out and try to get him to come in the house, to join us. Jimmy and I tried to answer his questions about God, but we really didn't know what to say to help him. I remember sitting in the yard that summer hearing the horn, far away on the dirt roads, like a sad echo of the harmonica music my Uncle Don used to play. As the summer wore on we all just wanted the horn to stop blowing.

The horn did stop blowing one night in September. Don took a rifle and went up the long hill toward the barn. He went into one of the old mine shacks, lay down on the floor, put the rifle in his mouth and pulled the trigger.

When his family woke up the next morning, everything was quiet. The truck was sitting in the driveway and Don was nowhere to be found. His Mom went to look for him, climbing that hill, maybe led by some mysterious tie a mother always has with her children. She didn't stop at the barn, didn't even glance in the door. Her feet took her right to the mining shack where she went in and found her son lying there on the floor.

I don't know how she made it back down that hill to tell her husband and Buster what had happened. I don't know what happened immediately after that, but I do know that later the phone calls went out to all of the family, phone calls that changed all of our lives forever.

When Don killed himself, Dana left her teaching job in Fresno, and never taught again in California.

Bob finished out his year of teaching in Davenport, but at the end of the school year he and his wife, Phyllis, left Davenport and moved to the farm to help the family. They lived with Buster and Grandma for quite a while. Then they bought John and Dorothy's farm, which was just down the road from Grandpa's farm. Bob taught in Knoxville for part of that time, but they eventually left the area and Bob returned to his teaching career.

Some of the joy of life seemed to leave Buster. He was terribly anxious and sad for a long time after Don's death. He went to a local doctor and started taking pills for his nerves.

Grandpa's hair turned white overnight. He died shortly after his son, Don.

My mother spent seven months in the psychiatric hospital in Iowa City. Luckily our family doctor in Washington, Iowa recognized the signs of depression and moved quickly to get her admitted.

Most of all I think we all felt, and still feel to some extent, a terrible sense of guilt. We didn't know what to do, and never sought professional help. I know now that this did not have to happen, that Don's life could have been saved if we had only known what to do.

The endless questions remain. What happened to bring about such a dramatic and sudden change in Don? Did he see something? Did he do something? There have never been any answers. So we lived, and still live, with the senseless loss of Don.

I have always felt that Don's death ended my childhood. The long happy summers, summers where I felt wrapped in the love of my beloved Agans were over.

THE DAY THE HORN STOPPED HONKING
By Barbara Paulding

He is not in his bed.
His seat at the breakfast table remains empty.

She pushes
Her hair back
Walks out into the yard
Eyes searching
Only the chickens are visible
Early morning September sun
Warm on their feathers

Edna walks slowly up the rutted path toward the barn
Her steps heavy
With her weight?
Dread?

She passes the barn
Barely glancing at the cows
Gathered for morning milking
Continues on, drawn always up
Up to the old mine shack

She pauses outside the door
Breathing heavily
Pushes it open
Leans against the side for support

At first glance he looks all right
Like he is sleeping
But she sees the blood that has pooled at the back of his head
The rifle still lying across his body

Does she scream?
Cry out?
See him at two, black hair dancing in the wind?
Clinging to her skirts as she hangs up the clothes?
Wish him safe, still in her belly?

MY MOTHER'S BROTHER: BOB AGAN

Bob, the youngest of the Agan boys, ran true to form. He was tall, dark and very handsome, maybe the best looking of all of the Agan men. He was so adorable as a little boy that the teachers usually favored him, but I'm sure Bob would have done just fine without all that extra attention. He was very smart and always had his nose in a book, reading everything he could get his hands on.

Although Bob worked at a lot of physically demanding jobs as he grew up, his life took a different path from that of his brothers. When Bob graduated from high school he enrolled in the Iowa State Teachers College in Cedar Falls. (Now University of Northern Iowa) He managed to work his way through college and was the first person in his family to graduate. While he was in college, our house in Deep River was his home, the place he came to on weekends and holidays.

Bob Agan, Tommy Paulding, and Dana Agan

Once when he was home, his friend Bobby Coker was at our house and they went outside to play catch. Bobby Coker was playing semi pro ball and was a great pitcher. He was throwing balls to Bob when something happened to his arm. Bobby Coke's arm was broken. It turned out that he had some kind of bone disease and had to quit playing baseball. That really hit Bob hard. Bob had always loved baseball and he and his friend Bobby had played together all through high school.

While he was a student at the Iowa State Teachers College he met a young man, Max McQue, and they became lifelong friends. Sometimes Max came home with Bob on weekends. When Bob and McQue graduated from college they both taught for my dad in Deep River. They stayed at our house during that school year.

Bob Agan on Deep River Main Street

My mom had Bob and Mac sleep in my brother, Jimmy's, room. The first night they stayed in that room, when they turned out the lights, they thought they had gone crazy. When they looked up at the ceiling they saw a bright moon and hundreds of stars. They finally realized my brother had put dozens of glow in the dark stars on his ceiling.

Bob read every night, lying in bed, reading his books, and munching crackers. Our house started to fill up with his "book of the month" selections. As soon as Bob was through with them I would start reading them. I'm sure some of the selections were not appropriate for a young child. *Strange Woman* comes to mind, but no one censored my reading.

Like most of the Agans, Bob was not religious, but he did agree to take my brother Jimmy to a revival meeting one night. After about ten minutes Bob had had enough and told Jimmy they had to go. As they walked out of the tent the minister called to them and said, "It's awfully dark out there boys, awfully dark." After that experience, Bob and Jimmy spent a lot more time hunting than going to revival meetings!

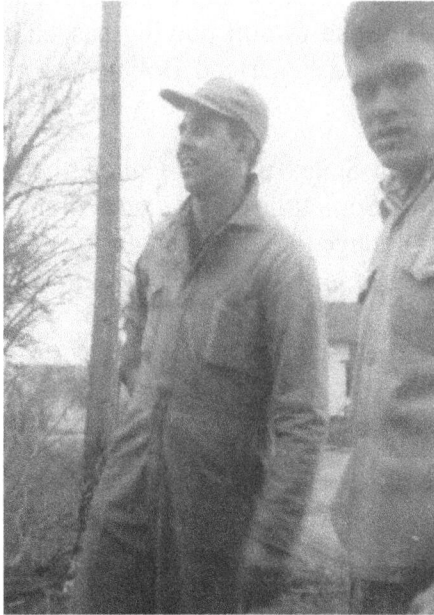

Bob Agan and Jimmy Paulding Going Pheasant Hunting

Bob met his wife, Phyllis, while he was teaching at Deep River. Phyllis was a high school student and when she graduated, she and Bob started dating. I remember Bob and Phyllis dancing at the open air dance floor in Deep River. During the summer a band came to town every Saturday night and the dance floor quickly filled up with couples twirling to the music. I thought Bob and Phyllis were always the handsomest couple on the dance floor. During this time Bob's taste in music switched from "Railroad Bill" to popular romantic songs like "Paper Doll".

Phyllis Gabriel Agan

Bob and Phyllis married, and after they left Deep River, Bob taught in many different schools. He spent some time in Scott's Bluff, Nebraska and also taught for a time in New Mexico. During his teaching career he went back to school and earned his Masters and Ph.D. in education. Bob became a school administrator and ended his career in Davenport, Iowa. His best friend, Max McQue also taught in Davenport until he retired.

Bob and Phyllis had three children, Dan, Chuck and Nancy. Bob was very proud of all of them. Both of the boys played baseball and Bob spent a lot of time with them.

Bob, Baby Chuck, and Dan Agan   *Chuck, Nancy, and Dan Agan*

After he and Phyllis left the farm in Marion County, they always lived in town. But Bob still kept a little bit of the farming life in his heart.

Bob chewed tobacco and liked to drive around with his window rolled down, spitting tobacco juice out the window. One day my dad told him he was going to ruin the paint on his car if he didn't stop getting tobacco juice all over the door. Bob just grinned and said, "I paid for the damn car, I guess I can ruin the paint job if I want to."

Bob had a big impact on my life. I am very grateful to the uncle with the books. Many of the books I read helped expand my horizons. I still have some of his books: *Gentleman's Agreement*, *The Grapes of Wrath,* and *Kingsblood Royal*. These books helped shape my world view and reinforced my very liberal outlook on life.

Thank you, Bob.

MY MOTHER'S SISTER: DANA RUTH AGAN

Dana was the youngest of the Agan children, and was my mother's only sister. She was a beautiful baby and grew into a beautiful young woman. She had the classic Agan looks, black hair, dark skin and brown eyes.

When she was very young she was diagnosed with curvature of the spine. Dana was fitted with a brace and the doctor instructed her to wear it every day. She was just entering her teen years, and like most young girls, she was desperate to fit in, to feel attractive. She started to ignore the doctor's orders and stopped wearing the brace to school. I don't know if wearing the brace everyday would have straightened her back, but as a result of her decision, her curvature got a little worse. I know Dana was always very self-conscious about her condition but you couldn't tell anything was wrong with her. She was simply breathtakingly beautiful.

Like the other children in the family, Dana's early years were not easy. Poverty was a constant factor, a gaping wound that never quite healed. Dana described many days when the only thing she and Bob had to eat was cold mush.

Dana's mother was still not taking very good care of her children, and was still ranting at her husband every night. To make matters worse for Dana and Bob, my mother, Thelma, was living away from home. Thelma had been all of the children's primary caretaker while she was living at home.

The Agans left Iowa right before Dana's senior year in high school. George took his family to Lawrence, Kansas, looking for work. Dana enrolled in high school in Lawrence, but she was overwhelmed by the large urban school. She contacted my parents and was soon on a train headed back to southern Iowa. We were living in Cantril at the time, and Dana came to live with us to finish her schooling.

Jimmy & Barbara Paulding with Dana Agan

Dana shared a room with me. She was a senior, and I was in first grade. Here was this beautiful teenager, who I worshipped, living with us. I remember so many things from that year. Every morning when we got ready for school, Dana took the time to lay over the bed, letting her head hang over the edge. "This makes your cheeks rosy," she would tell me. I always watched while she fixed her hair for the day. Those beauty rituals usually meant we were running late. Dana would grab my hand and pull me down the sidewalk to school. She always waited for me and walked me home after school. One day I watched as she rescued my brother, Jimmy, when some older boys were threatening to beat him up.

I loved having her there, living with us.

When she graduated from high school she followed her brother Bob to Iowa State Teachers College in Cedar Falls. She was the second person in her family to graduate from college. While she was in college she came to our house on breaks and the occasional weekend. When she graduated she went to California to join her parents and brothers. She started her teaching career in California and always credited the California school system for helping her become such a great teacher. At that time, all new teachers in California worked under an experienced teacher for a full year.

Dana had a very happy life in California. She loved teaching, learned to ski and spent many weekends on the slopes. She later told me, "I was never very good, but I always had a lot of fun."

She also started dating a young doctor. She always came home to the farm in the summer and I loved those days when I was there with her. She often read me the letters she got from her doctor.

Dana Agan in California

Like everyone else in the family, Dana's life completely changed when Don killed himself. Of course she came home from California and then, when her dad got so sick, she stayed in Iowa.

During these terrible times Merle Bolton started coming to the farm to see Dana. Merle was a sergeant in the army and he and Dana started dating. The doctor in California continued to write to Dana and wanted to come to Iowa to be with her. Dana told him, "No, absolutely not." When I asked her why she said, "I can't let him see how my family lives." She told me this while we were upstairs in the old farm house, my favorite place in the world. She could see that I didn't understand so she added, "Barbara, you've never had to worry when someone comes to your house. The house is always clean, the sheets are fresh, the dishes are always done. You don't know what it's like to be ashamed of how your parents live." I still didn't understand but I knew then that her doctor would never come to Iowa to see her.

Dana's dad died in November and Dana married her soldier in early December at a church in Bussey. I begged my parents to take me, but my mother had traveled too far down the road to depression to make the trip.

Cliff Bolton, Maggie Bolton, Merle Bolton, Dana Agan Bolton, Edna Agan, Buster Agan

The summer after they got married, Merle was stationed in California. Grandma and Buster were also in California, in the Modesto area. Our family traveled out west too, and spent the summer in Modesto. I was able to spend a week near the ocean with Dana and Merle. Dana and I went to the beach almost every day. She was pregnant so she mainly watched me swim while she sat on the beach and soaked up the sun. At the end of the summer we went back to Iowa while Dana and Merle went to Japan.

Merle Bolton & Dana Bolton in California Before Leaving for Japan

Dana had a baby girl, Debbie, while she was in Japan.

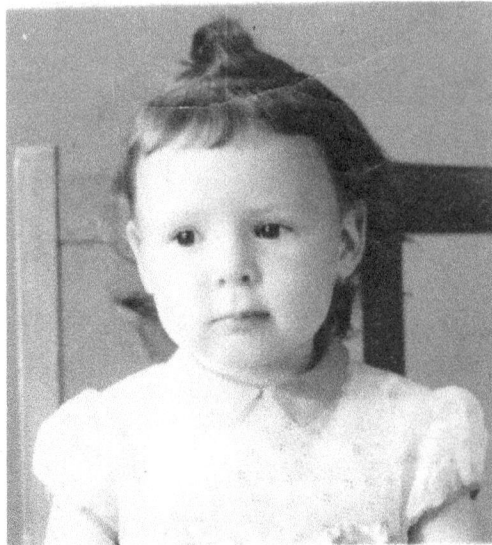

Debbie Bolton

When we got the news that they were coming home, we all went to the farm to welcome them back. I was in my first year of college. Buster told me to hide behind the door on the stairs. He was planning to tell Dana I wasn't there.

When Dana, Merle, and Debbie came in everyone was talking at once. They all sounded so happy! Then I heard Dana ask, "Where's Barbara? Isn't she here?" I opened the stair door and went into the room, thinking I would see my beautiful Dana again. Instead I saw a stranger, a person so thin and emaciated, it made me think of a concentration camp victim. I wanted to cry but I didn't, I just hugged her close.

Dana told me later that if it hadn't been for Merle's commanding officer, she and Debbie would have starved. Merle spent all of his pay on liquor and women. There was never any food in the house. The officer brought Dana groceries, sometimes on a daily basis. When he saw that things were not getting better, he arranged for Merle to be sent back to the states.

When Dana and Merle came back to the states, they lived at the farm with Buster and Grandma. Two years after Debbie was born, Dana had another little red haired daughter, Cindy. Things did not get any better for Dana's marriage, but she was protected from the worst of Merle's behavior by her family. Buster saw to it that there was always plenty of food in the house.

When Cindy was almost a year old, Dana decided to leave Merle. She planned to come to our house in Cotter to live until she could get a teaching job. In December, 1955, Buster, Dana, Grandma, Debbie and Cindy got in Buster's pickup, and headed for our house. On highway 92, just outside of Washington, Iowa, a young driver crossed the center line and slammed into the truck. Buster, Grandma, Dana, and Debbie were all fine. Cindy wasn't. She was taken to the University of Iowa Hospital, where she died from massive head injuries. They were only about fourteen miles from our house, from safety.

I don't know how Dana managed to recover from another senseless tragedy. I will never know how people survive the loss of a child.

After Cindy's funeral, Dana decided to give her marriage one more chance and returned to Merle. I think Merle may have tried for a while, but things soon went downhill. After her son, Jeff, was born Dana left again, once more coming to our house. Jeff was about six months old when they came to live with us for the summer.

At the end of the summer Dana went to Davenport to teach for her brother, Bob, who was a principle in the Davenport school system.

When she left Davenport, and went to Des Moines to teach, she and the kids moved in with Buster and her mother. They rented a small house on Dubuque Street and then eventually bought a beautiful home in Pleasant Hill. Dana loved that house.

Dana and Debbie Bolton

Dana and Jeff Bolton

Dana continued to teach until she had a stroke when she was in her fifties. She was a very dedicated teacher and was appointed assistant principle at Garfield Elementary School.

Dana loved her kids and grandkids, loved teaching, loved dancing, horse racing, and the Chicago Cubs. She was fiercely liberal, a lifelong democrat and a prolific "letter to the editor" writer. Most of her letters were published!

Dana was my aunt, my idol, and more importantly my lifelong friend. She had a big impact on my life, as a child and as an adult. I still miss her.

MY MOTHER'S EXTENDED FAMILY: THE AGANS

MY MOTHER'S GRANDMA AND GRANDPA AGAN

Lewis Agan, my mother's grandpa, married a young woman named Mary Nancy Williamson. They began their married life on the eighty acre farm Lewis' father gave him. The farm was located on Agan Ridge, not far from Gosport.

Lewis and Mary had eight children: Nancy Viola, Kathleen, John, George (my mother's dad), Elise, the twins: Earl and Clarice Pearl, and Stephen (who everyone called Pete). Elise died when she was thirteen, and Earl's twin sister, Clarice Pearl, died in infancy. The other children all grew to adulthood,

I never knew my Great Grandfather Lewis. He died when my mother was nine years old. Most of the stories I heard about him centered on his love of farming and his kindness to his children.

I did know my Great Grandma Mary Agan and I loved her. Great Grandma lived with her daughter Kate in Montana during the winter months, but every summer she came home to Iowa. She had to leave Iowa in the winter to avoid catching pneumonia. When she came home to Iowa she always went to her oldest son, John's, house. John lived on the farm where she and Lewis had lived, where they had raised their children. For some reason she never stayed at John's for very long. After a few days Great Grandma would get word to my dad that she wanted to come to our house, so Dad would go get her. She always stayed with us the whole summer, sometimes into early October. When she arrived at our house she would usually tell my mom, "John won't let me do anything. He thinks I should just sit in a rocking chair." She loved to work. Dad always let her feed the chickens and pigs. Great Grandma also wanted to milk the cows but Dad was afraid that she would get hurt doing that. Later in life, he told me many times that he should have let her milk the cows.

Mary Nancy Williamson Agan

My great grandma loved my mom. The two of them worked side by side in the house, sharing all of the chores. While she was there she always made her famous ammonia cookies. I have never been able to find a recipe for those cookies. Even my mom didn't know how to make them.

I shared a room with my great grandma and I remember watching her get ready for the day, carefully fixing her long, beautiful white hair.

Great Grandma really knew her livestock. One summer evening as she was looking out the window she said, "Jim, you've got a sick chicken out there. You better take care of it so the others don't get sick." So, Dad went out and killed a chicken. When he came back in the house she looked out again, shook her head and said, "Jim, you killed the wrong chicken."

Sometimes she and Dad would sit on the back porch and have an apple peeling contest. Whoever got the longest, continuous peel won. It probably seems strange in today's world to think that such simple things could bring us so much pleasure.

Great Grandma was one of the kindest people to inhabit my young world. I always had a vivid imagination and my days were filled with imaginary friends and creatures. The Hussins lived in the old boxelder tree in our back yard and were always looking for bread to feed to their tiny babies. Then there was the "Little German Girl" who sometimes showed up to play with me. The Little German Girl especially loved cookies. Great Grandma always gave me bread for the Hussins and at least one extra cookie for the "Little German Girl." One day she asked me how all of these critters liked their food. I told her I knew that they loved it because when I went back to check on the food, it was always gone.

I loved to play school. When I told Great Grandma, "I wish I had some students." She smiled and said, "Well, we can fix that."

She showed me how to take the chickens, tuck their heads under their wings, and give them one "turn on the merry go round." After their ride, they would sit still for their lessons. She even convinced my mother to let me bring them into the kitchen and sit them on my little chairs for their daily lessons. I don't know how she managed that because my mother never let me bring any animals into the house.

Great Grandma died when I was five. My parents would not let me go to her funeral so I never really got to say good bye. She is buried at home, in the Gosport cemetery, next to her husband Lewis.

I still have a quilt she made for my mom and I have all of my memories. She was a wonderful Great Grandma.

SCHOOL
By Barbara Paulding

You let me bring
Them into
The kitchen

Four fat hens

I line up the
Little chairs
Sit them down
In their seats

Sometimes they
Rustle their
Feathers

Lift their wings
Tentatively

I scold them
Tell them to behave
Sit still
Until recess

MY MOTHER'S AUNT KATE

Aunt Kate married a rancher and lived out west near Billings, Montana. When her father died, Aunt Kate took her mother with her to live her on the ranch. Every year, when she brought Great Grandma back to Iowa, we would have a brief visit with her. She was a tall, straight person, a no nonsense type of woman.

After Great Grandma died I don't believe Aunt Kate returned to Iowa until my Grandpa, her younger brother, passed away. She was seven years older than my Grandpa, in her early seventies, but she managed to make the trip back to Iowa for his funeral. She stayed at the farm during that time and she seemed to be a source of stability and comfort. A few days after my grandpa's funeral she returned to Montana.

That was the last time I saw my Great Aunt Kate.

MY MOTHER'S UNCLE EARL

My mother's Uncle Earl died in 1935, two years before I was born. Even though I never met him I felt like I knew him. He was the only one of my mother's relatives people told stories about. Like most family stories, some were true, others were pure fiction.

My dad always told me, "If you want to know what Uncle Earl was like, just look at Buster. He looks like Earl and he has that same personality."

Earl Agan

Earl was tall, dark and handsome and more than a little on the wild side.

Uncle Earl was known as a drinker, a gambler and a bootlegger. I believe all of these stories were probably true. He started selling bootleg whiskey during prohibition but continued after the ban on alcohol was lifted. Because of these activities, Earl was frequently in the Marion County jail. My dad liked to tell the story about the night he and Buster went to the jail in Knoxville to see Earl. When they went in, the sheriff told them Earl wasn't there, they had let him out so he could go sell his whiskey. The sheriff assured them that Earl would be back soon!

Because of his bootleg business, Earl was one of the few Agans who had ready cash. When my mother was ready to graduate from Knoxville High School she was stunned to find out that the cost of attending graduation, and receiving her graduation picture, would be fifty dollars. It might as well have been fifty thousand. When Earl heard about her problem he gave my mother the fifty dollars so she could walk proudly down the aisle in her gown and, more importantly, pay for her beautiful graduation picture.

While Earl was still living at home on Agan Ridge, he frequently went to the Gosport school to pick up the younger children. He met the new school teacher, Ollie Evans, and started spending time with her. Ollie got pregnant, which was a big scandal in those days, and of course Earl married her. Earl and Ollie were married in 1923. The story my mother always told me was that after he married Ollie he took her to his mother's house and never lived with her. As it turns out, this story wasn't true. Earl and Ollie did live together. They had a small farm in Marion County, and were together until Earl died in 1935.

Ollie Evans Agan

They didn't just have one baby, they had two daughters, Virginia and Dorthea. Virginia never married. She became a school teacher, and when she retired, she returned to Hamilton where she built a new house next to the big quarry. Dorthea married William Bolton and had six children and many grandchildren.

Virginia & Dorthea Agan

So Earl has many decedents, some undoubtedly living today. I'm very glad that as an adult, I got to know their daughter, Virginia, and learned the truth about my great uncle Earl and his wife, Ollie.

Ollie Agan with Grandson Bobby

After Earl died, Ollie left the farm and moved to Hamilton. She was appointed postmistress in 1940 and held that position until she retired in 1950. As a little girl living in Hamilton, I clearly remember running to the post office to get the mail or buy stamps and penny post cards. I remember Ollie as a large, gentle woman who always had a kind word for me and who could usually find a sucker in one of the drawers. During all of that time I never knew that she was my great aunt. I wish I would have known that this very kind woman was related to me, that she was my great aunt Ollie.

MY MOTHER'S UNCLE PETE

Uncle Pete was the youngest of the Agan children. He did not look much like the other Agan boys. He was short, dark-haired, and somewhat wizened.

Bob Agan (in car) John Agan, & Uncle Stephen "Pete" Agan

My Dad told me that Pete was the best checker player in Marion County. He used to play at the corner store in Gosport and nobody could beat him. I think Pete lived in Knoxville most of his life. To my knowledge he never married.

Sometimes when we were visiting my grandpa's farm, Pete would come in the house in the middle of the night and would go behind the couch to sleep. When we woke up in the morning, there he would be! I don't remember Pete ever sleeping anywhere except behind the couch.

Pete was very kind to all of us and he usually brought us bananas to eat. In his later years he was somewhat famous for walking around Knoxville giving bananas to the children. I don't know how he made his living or why he was so fond of bananas!

Pete died when he was in his sixties.

MY MOTHER'S EXTENDED FAMILY: THE CROYS

MY MOTHERS GRANDPA AND GRANDMA CROY

Martin Croy and Lucinda Ellen Hunt Croy had eight living children: Ansel, Edna, (my Mom's Mother), Homer, Grace, Bryan, Pearl, Clarence, and Glenn. A son and daughter died in infancy. They had a thousand acre farm near Gosport.

Lucinda Croy on the 1000 acre farm (Pearl Croy in background)

Martin Croy and Lucinda seemed to have had a good life up until the time Martin died in 1918. My mother was just six years old when he died.

When Martin died, his eldest son, Ansel, inherited the family farm. He married, had a family, and moved his mother, Lucinda, into a small house in Melcher. After Lucinda left the farm, Ansel started gambling the farm away.

When my mother was very young, she was sometimes sent to the farm to help Ansel's wife. She worked very hard and was only paid two dollars a week.

After Grandma Croy moved to Melcher, she met a man named Parr Huxford and they got married. Grandma Croy was a big woman and Parr was a small, thin man. As a child I remember thinking they were like the old nursery rhyme, Jack Sprat.

Parr Huxford & Lucinda Croy Huxford

We visited them frequently when I was very young, and I always knew Grandma Croy by her new name, Grandma Huxford. I thought Parr was wonderful. He had real marionettes and would always get them out and put on a show for my brother, Jimmy, and me.

I think Grandma Croy was very happy during the years she was married to Parr.

THE CROY BOYS

I can't remember my mother's uncles on the Croy side. I'm sure they were at some of the annual Agan/Croy reunions we had every summer in Knoxville, but I have absolutely no memory of them.

The stories I heard were mainly about Ansel, the oldest son, and Glenn, the baby of the family. The stories about Ansel were mostly about his gambling and how he lost the family's thousand acre farm.

Clarence & Georgia Croy on the 1000 acre farm

The stories about Glenn were all about a baby who was cherished and loved, a baby born with a major physical problem.

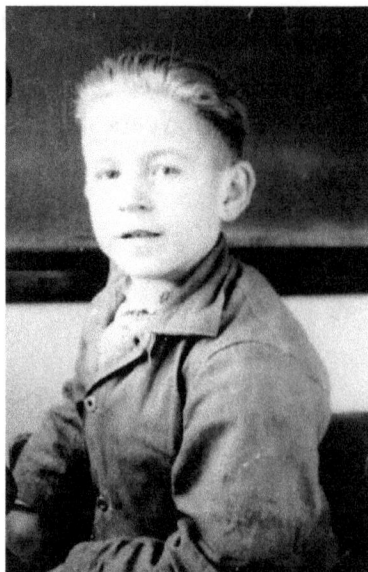

Glenn Croy

When Glenn was born his knees were on backwards. His parents took him to many doctors but were told there was nothing that could be done until he finished growing. My dad said he got around really well by walking on his hands.

Glenn Croy on the Porch at the 1000 Acre Farm

When he was a teenager they operated and Glenn learned to walk. I have a little tin cup that was Glenn's baby cup. It has the word *darling* inscribed on one side. I think he was a very loved little boy.

Glenn Croy's Cups

MY MOTHER'S AUNT GRACE

Grace Croy

My mother had two aunts on the Croy side: Grace and Pearl.

Grace & Pearl Croy

Grace was much like her older sister, Edna, in looks and personality. She married Walter Goering, a successful farmer, and lived out her married life on Walter's farm, located just south of Knoxville.

Walter was a tall, thin man with a kind, sweet face. He was a very gentle, kind man. Grace and Walter had one son, Marvin, He married a young woman named Stella and they had four daughters. These grandchildren brought a lot of joy to Grace and Walter.

Stella Goering & Baby, Grace Croy Goering, Edna Croy Agan, Don Agan, Walter Goering, George Agan, Buster Agan, Marvin Goering's Three Girls on Walter's Farm

I remember Grace and Walter as being two of the kindest people I knew.

Walter & Grace Goering

When they were farming they sold cream and eggs in Knoxville. My mother used to talk about scooping the cream out of a bowl for her cereal. She said the cream was too thick to pour!

Like her older sister, Edna, Grace gave warm, wonderful hugs. She was a great cook. When we had our annual reunions she always brought a creamy lemon desert, a desert I have never been able to find a recipe for.

Grace and Walter were very frugal. They never charged anything. They always paid cash for their purchases, even their new cars.

They are buried in the Knoxville Cemetery.

Grace & Walter Goering

MY MOTHER'S AUNT PEARL

Pearl Croy was the youngest girl in the family. She differed from her sisters physically. Edna and Grace were both large women. Pearl was always thin, determined to stay that way, and somewhat vain about her figure. Like all of the Croy children Pearl attended school at Gosport.

Pearl's Class at Gosport School

Pearl was a very popular girl. She had a lot of admirers and they all corresponded with her, sending her many postcards and letters. She was usually addressed as kiddo, kid, midget, etc. Some of the cards from her admirers were quite risqué for the times!

Postcard to Pearl Croy

Eventually Pearl fell in love with a neighboring farmer's son, Harmon Klootwyk. During their courtship Harmon enlisted in the army and fought in World War One.

Harmon Klootwyk

Pearl Croy & Harmon Klootwyk

They wrote each other many letters and post cards during the time Harmon was away. I still have those letters. In one, Harmon describes being forced to watch the army hang two men for desertion at Camp Dodge.

CAMP DODGE IOWA SUNDAY, JULY 7, 1918

Dear friend Pearl,

My arm is still pretty sore from all of the shots. All the new recruits were vaccinated again yesterday. We will get one more vaccination, that will be next Saturday I suppose. I sure will be glad when it is all over with, for it goes pretty hard on us. Some of the boys faint...

There were five boy discharged from our company, wish I was one of them. I suppose you folks read in the paper about those three negroes they hung up here. Well I seen all of it. I felt sorry for them at the time but I guess they got just what was coming to them. It seemed more like a 4th of July celebration to me than anything else, right after they sprung the traps bands began to play and most of them went to singing. The whole eighty eighth division was out to see the hanging, besides three thousand negroes.

CAMP DODGE IOWA JULY18, 1918

Dear Friend Pearl,

Received your letter this morning and was sure glad to get it... Well how are you feeling these days? I am sure getting tired of my job up here, but I guess I will have to stick on as long as I last or till the war is over. It isn't near the life I thought it would be... There was another soldier skiffed out last night. He was on guard duty at night, left his post, went the barn, saddled him a horse and left. I suppose there will be another hanging when they catch him. Well I don't blame him if he thinks he can get away with it. But I would hate to take his chances... Sure getting tired of being shut up here...

CAMP DODGE IOWA JULY 31, 1918

Dear Friend Pearl,

Well as I have a little spare time will try and write you a few lines... Well I had a pretty good little friend when I was walking my post. There was a little dog followed me all night. They had eleven prisoners in the guard house. They were sure a sober looking bunch... I think our time here is getting short. Company M349 left today and we are next... There were four boys killed themselves here in the last two days. One of them just near my next door shot himself this morning Well I believe I would rather let somebody else have a chance at mine... I wish I could see you once more for I left...

That was Harmon's last letter from Camp Dodge. Of course the letters kept coming, from New York, England and France. Once he left Camp Dodge his letters were all censored, some had many sections that were actually cut from the pages. Harmon's greetings changed as his time away from home dragged on and on. Before he shipped overseas, his letters were addressed to "Dear Friend Pearl." In contrast, the letters from France are addressed to "Sweetheart" and usually signed "Your loving Harmon."

When Harmon returned from the war he and Pearl got married and lived on a farm south of Knoxville.

Harmon & Pearl Klootwyk Wedding Picture   *Harmon & Pearl Klootwyk on Their Farm*

Harmon raised hogs and was very successful. I remember Harmon as a large man with a round, flushed face. He was always jolly when we saw him at family gatherings, but my mother said that he and Pearl had some terrible arguments. She lived with them for a year when she was teaching at Gosport and she said she witnessed many fights. Once I guess Pearl threw a butcher knife at Harmon and just barely missed him! Pearl and Harmon didn't have any children but they were always good to their many nieces and nephews.

When Harmon quit farming they bought a house in Knoxville. Harmon died at their home in Knoxville after shoveling snow. Pearl lived a long time after Harmon died. She became very interested in religion and enjoyed the sermons she watched on television.

Pearl Klootwyk at her House in Knoxville

A few years after Harmon died, Pearl decided to move into a nursing home in Knoxville. She was still in good health and her mind was fine, but she just decided that was what she wanted. She spent her last days in the nursing home, helping the other residents.

Pearl and Harmon are buried in the Gosport Cemetery.

MY MOTHER: THELMA ETHYL AGAN

My mom, Thelma, was born on February 6, 1912 somewhere in Marion County. When she came along her older brother, John, was just two years old. Her brothers, Buster, Don and Bob, soon followed. Then, when my mom was fourteen, she finally had a little sister, Dana. All of her brothers and her sister loved and admired my mom. They never called her Thelma, she was always "Sis."

When my mom started school, she was often teased about her red hair and freckles. Some of the older children even teased her about her dad, asking who her daddy really was. Did this make her question her own parentage? I think there was a time in her life when she probably wondered if George was her father. However, as she got older, when she looked in the mirror, she could clearly see her father's features in her own face.

My mom had a very difficult childhood. From an early age she had to do most of the housework, cooking, and had to take care of all of her younger siblings. She grew up working hard and never stopped.

She had a lifelong dream to finish high school and to become a teacher. The odds were not in her favor. Her family lived far from Knoxville and she was definitely needed at home. Her dad had always depended on her to provide some stability in the home.

When she graduated from eighth grade at Gosport she moved to Melcher Dallas to be closer to the high school in Knoxville. She moved in with her Grandma Croy, but that arrangement didn't last long. When Grandma Croy's sons came to town, asking to move in with her, Grandma Croy told my mom she would have to leave.

My mom contacted her Aunt Grace, who lived even closer to Knoxville, and Aunt Grace told her she would be welcome to live with them. So she moved to Aunt Grace and Uncle Walter's farm. Every day she left the house early and walked up the railroad tracks to school. She usually met a lot of miners while she was walking up the tracks. She said she was never afraid of the men, that they usually tipped their hats to her and wished her a good day.

Knoxville High School

In exchange for her room and board, Aunt Grace only asked one thing of my mom. Aunt Grace hated doing dishes but she loved to cook so she asked my mom if she would do the day's dishes when she got home. Mom agreed, so every evening when she came home from school there was a big sink full of dishes waiting for her!

Aunt Grace was very kind. When she found out my mom didn't have a winter coat, she made her a beautiful, warm winter coat. Mom wore the coat every day that winter.

Throughout her high school years her dad would frequently come and see her, telling her that she might have to quit school and come home and take care of the younger kids if things didn't get better. My mom felt very guilty about what was happening at home but she just couldn't give up her dreams. She stayed in school.

In her senior year she moved to Knoxville so that she wouldn't have to make the long walk to school from her aunt Grace's farm.

Knoxville Square

She lived with the Hedrick family where she worked for her room and board, helping Mrs. Hedrick with the children and housework. The Hedrick's owned the dry cleaning establishment in Knoxville. My mom always said that the Hedrick family "saved her." I think after all of her struggles, life with the Hendricks must have seemed like a godsend. They were all very good to her. Mrs. Hedrick gave her many of her own clothes, and when it was time for Mom to graduate she bought a new dress and pair of shoes for Mom to wear. That was her first new dress and pair of shoes.

Thelma Agan's Graduation Picture

One time during her senior year she and a friend applied for part time work with one of the doctors who lived at the Knoxville Veterans Hospital. It was a Saturday job and didn't interfere with the work she did for the Hedrick's. She only worked there for one day. The doctor made inappropriate advances and she immediately quit.

When my mom graduated, she had completed all of her normal training classes. If she could pass her test she could begin teaching. The Normal Training Teachers Test was not an easy one, but she passed it with flying colors.

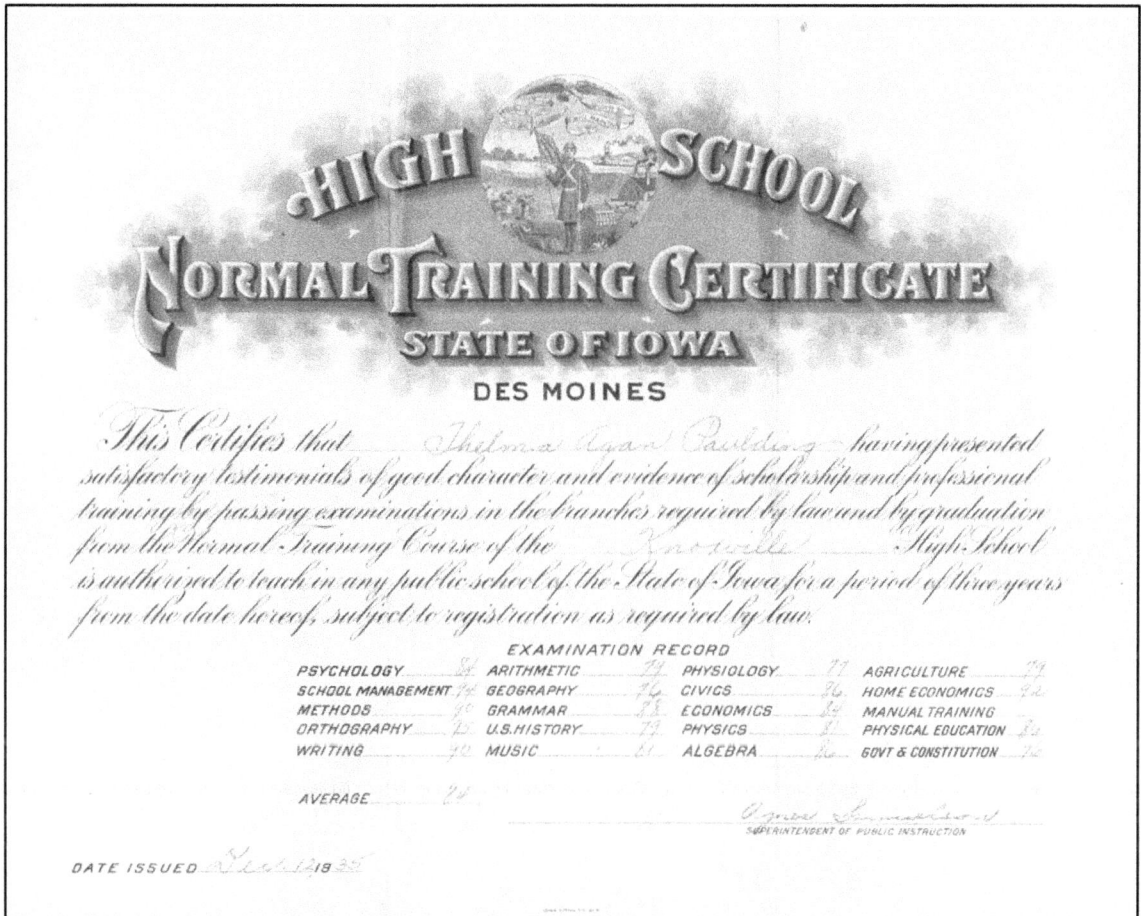

Thelma Agan's Normal Training Certificate

Mom started her teaching career at Gosport, the little country school she had attended as a child. While she taught at Gosport she lived with her Aunt Pearl and Uncle Harmon.

During this time her parents moved to Hamilton, right across the alley from Jimmy Paulding's house. That is where she met Jimmy, her future husband. Jimmy saw her in the yard, washing her family's old car, walked over, and asked her for a date. She said no, but that night when Jimmy was walking down the street toward church she caught up to him and took his hand. She held his hand all through the church service and they were married three years later.

When my mom got engaged she was teaching sixth, seventh, and eighth grade at the elementary school in Columbia. This was the first time she had taught in a "town school." She was very proud of the Columbia school. It had two rooms; the younger children were in one room, the sixth, seventh and eighth graders were in another.

When the children heard that their teacher was getting married, their parents made a beautiful quilt for them. The quilt has a picture of the Columbia School in the middle with the date of their marriage. Around the center are the names of all the children Mom taught that year. I still have that quilt.

Columbia School

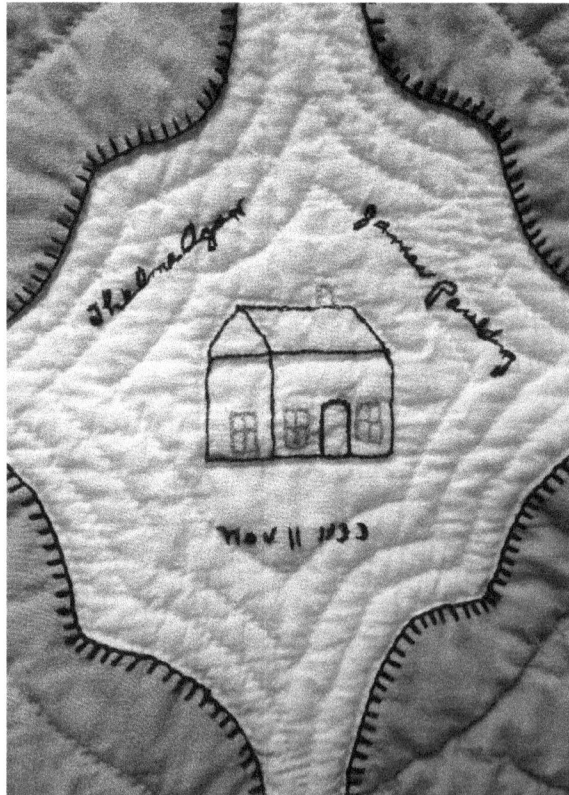

Thelma Agan & Jim Paulding's Wedding Quilt

My parents were married on November 11, 1933. Mom's Aunt Pearl and her brother, Buster, stood up for them. They were married in Knoxville by a justice of the peace. My dad had purchased a simple, white gold wedding ring for my mom. They spent their wedding night at Pearl and Harmon's farm. The next day Mom returned to Columbia to teach, and my dad went back to Hamilton to teach at Marysville. For the rest of the school year they only saw each other on weekends. When they finished the school year, they moved to Hamilton and bought a little camp house, which was always called "The Little Black House."

My older brother Jimmy and I were both born at home in the Little Black House. It was just down the block from both of their parents' homes. Mom quit teaching when Jimmy was born and became a full time mother and homemaker.

Jim, Thelma, Barb, and Jimmy Paulding at the Little Black House

My parents had to leave Hamilton when I was about two years old. My dad always said they had to move because they had "eaten their house." This was during the depression and jobs were very hard to come by. Like many families, my parents had to go to Faye Snack's store and charge groceries. When their bill reached $250.00 Faye Snack figured that was about what their house was worth and told them she would take their house in exchange for their debt. Faye accumulated a lot of real estate that way. Even though it was hard to leave their home, Faye Snack's willingness to let my parents charge all of those groceries was a blessing.

We moved to Centerville and my dad worked for Dwight Vredenburg in his grocery store. It was the first of many stores Dwight owned, and his stores eventually became an extremely successful enterprise called Hy-Vee. Dad also worked at the CCC camp in Centerville, teaching English to young Italian workers.

We lived in an upstairs apartment in Centerville, where my mom said we almost froze to death in the winters. At night we all had to sleep in one bed where we covered ourselves with every blanket we owned.

Barb and Jimmy in Centerville

Thelma, Jimmy, and Barb in Centerville

While Dad was working for Dwight he usually brought home a big bag of ginger snaps on Friday nights. I think the cookies cost a nickel. We sometimes got to go to the movies on the weekend. Our whole family got into the movies for a dime. They were held outside and I remember all of us sitting on long wooden benches while we watched the magic on the big screen.

After we left Centerville we moved around frequently. Times slowly got better and my Dad could usually find work as a school teacher and administrator. One of my favorite places was the little coal mining town of Pershing. This is where my Great Grandma Agan came to visit us, where the Hussins and the Little German Girl lived.

Jim, Thelma, Barb, and Jimmy Paulding in Pershing

The year before I was to start school, my mom made many beautiful little dresses for me. At that time when you bought feed for your animals, the feed came in cloth bags. Many of the feed sacks had beautiful patterns on them and Mom used these to make my dresses. She was a beautiful seamstress and always added special touches to my clothes, such as bits of lace or ribbons. She also sewed many little dresses for my old, cracked doll, Portia. Portia got her name from one of the soap operas Mom listened to on the radio. Her favorite soap operas were Stella Dallas, Backstage Wife, and Portia Faces Life. Portia was her favorite. While we lived in Pershing we listened to all of them every afternoon while she was cooking supper or finishing up some of the housework.

Pershing School

As things improved financially, Mom found herself faced with new challenges. When I was twelve my Dad had a "nervous breakdown" and was unable to teach for over a year. We still owned a house in Deep River, so our family moved back there. Dad tried to sell tools for the Albert Lee Tool Company, but he was not a very good salesman.

Jim Paulding and His Tool Truck

We soon found ourselves without enough money for food. My mom never complained, she just went to the nearby turkey factory and got a job. It was hard, unpleasant work but she never complained and never missed a day of work. The foreman always said she was the only woman who never swore and was always a lady. Because of her work we were able to make it through the year.

Dad recovered enough to start teaching again and we all moved to Cotter, Iowa. At the beginning of that school year, Mom's brother, Don, killed himself and her dad died shortly after that. She spent six months in the psychiatric hospital in Iowa City. We drove to Iowa City every night. While Dad went in to see her, Jimmy, Tommy, and I sat in the waiting room during visiting hours. We did not see our mother for the entire six months.

The summer after Mom got out of the hospital we all went to California. Her mom and her brother, Buster, were already in California. Dana and Merle were also there waiting for deployment to Japan. We went to Modesto, California but when we arrived we didn't have any money. We moved into Kruger's Auto Court and decided to try our luck at picking fruit in the valley. Kruger's Auto Court was an awful place. The floors were dirt and nothing was very clean. It was a place for the down and outers, for migrant workers. Mom never complained about it, just cleaned it up as best she could.

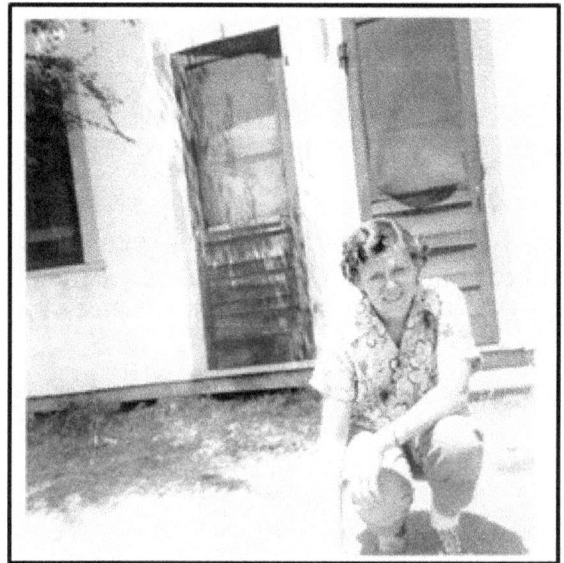

Tommy Paulding and Barbara Paulding at Kruger's Auto Court

We all got jobs picking fruit in the San Joaquin Valley. There were six of us working, so even though the pay was lousy, we made enough to pay rent and get groceries. Things weren't going too badly until one day my mother took her heavy boxes of fruit to be tallied for the day. The man looked at the boxes, looked at my mother, and pointed to a tall pile of boxed fruit. "Put it up there lady, put it up there and be quick about it." Mom put the boxes on the ground, her hands on her hips and said, "You put it up there!" And we all walked off the job. That was the end of our fruit picking career.

After we left the fields, my dad and older brother got good jobs building a canal. We rented a nice house and had a wonderful summer in California.

Jim Paulding (middle) with Co-workers Building Canal

When we got home from California, Mom started teaching again, took college classes, and eventually graduated from Iowa Wesleyan College.

Jim & Thelma Paulding at Thelma's College Graduation

During those years she had the unique experience of attending college with each of her three children. She was a great teacher and never missed a year until she retired in her sixties.

Thelma Paulding During Her Teaching Career

Thelma Paulding Reading to Children During Library Time

My parents were married for 74 years and seemed to love each other more as the years passed. When Mom was 95 she became very sick. The doctors were pretty sure she had pancreatic cancer. We took her to Mercy Hospital in Des Moines. When I brought Dad up to see her the next day she said, "There you are Jim. I couldn't find you anywhere." She took his hand and held on tight, just as she had so long ago when she took his hand as they walked to church in Hamilton.

Jim & Thelma Paulding on 60th Wedding Anniversary

My dad had a very peaceful, blessed passing. My mom had a very difficult, painful death. After the doctors had done all they could, we made arrangement to take Mom home to her house on the river. Hospice came and set everything up but unfortunately a big blizzard hit and delayed her homecoming for a few days. When she arrived at her house she was in a coma and I'm not sure if she ever knew she got to come home. We set her bed up in the living room, looking out on the river, the river where she used to watch the eagles in the winter.

Even with steady doses of morphine, Mom was in constant pain. I stayed there with Dad and got up every fifteen minutes to give her more morphine. Even with all of the medication you could tell she was in terrible pain. I don't remember how long she was home before she died. The days all blurred together with Mom always in pain and me always watching the clock, anxiously waiting for the fifteen minutes to be up so she could have more medicine. We played music constantly: Randy Travis and all of her favorite hymns. One afternoon I had to leave for about an hour to go to the doctor. My daughter, Beth, was there with Mom. She passed away while I was gone.

Mom died February 11, just six days after 96th birthday.

EPILOGUE

Thelma Ethyl Agan had a very difficult childhood and a very difficult death. But those two realities do not define her life.

When I think of my mother I think of her strength, determination, and grace. She faced life squarely and met every challenge with dignity. She had so many happy years while she and my dad were married.

After the children were raised, and the financial challenges were far behind them, they retired with no financial worries. In their later years they lived in a house on the Cedar River in Louisa County. Mom designed the house herself and two of their former students built it for them. She really loved that house.

Jim & Thelma Paulding at Their House on Cedar River

They had big gardens, a large strawberry patch, and Mom always grew prize winning flowers. She took up painting and made many beautiful pictures. She also continued to quilt and made sure all of the children and grandchildren each had one of her quilts. I think the last quilt she made was for her great grandson Joshua Michael.

Thelma Paulding Holding One of Her Many Quilts

For many years my parents left Iowa every winter and went to Hot Springs, Arkansas. Mother loved Hot Springs, it was like a second home to her. She and Dad would walk on the promenade and she loved taking the baths in the mineral water. During this time Bill Clinton was the Governor of Arkansas, and Bill and Hillary frequently came to Hot Springs. Like most Agans she was already a staunch Democrat, but having the chance to meet the Clintons and interact with them, solidified her support for them when Bill ran for president.

Thelma Paulding at Hotel in Hot Springs

Promenade at Hot Springs

Her life was full and happy even though she dealt with a lot of arthritic pain in her later years. She was always happy when her "kids" came to see her and never stopped loving and caring for all of us. Her grandchildren and great grandchildren enriched her latter years.

Thelma Paulding and Granddaughter Beth Goldstein

Four Generations: Beth Goldstein Burgmeyer, Barb Paulding, Thelma Paulding, and Abby Burgmeyer

If you have ever read the book, *Girl of The Limberlost*, you will surely remember the heroine, Elnora. This was one of Mom's favorite books. I always wondered if she was aware of the many similarities between Elnora's life and her own. Both had extremely difficult childhoods, both were determined to go to school, both had people who helped them out. During their senior years both lived with kind, giving people who helped them realize their dreams. Probably the biggest similarity I have always seen between my mom and Elnora is the way both young girls faced their difficulties with strength, dignity and grace.

If Thelma Ethyl Agan was like Elnora, she was also very much like her father, George Agan. She persevered.

APPENDIX

SONGS AND POEMS TOLD BY THE AGAN FAMILY.

Songs and Poems told to me by Edna Croy Agan

TWO LITTLE BOYS IN BLUE

Two little boys
Had two little toys
Each was a wooden horse

Gaily they played
Each summer day
Both were brave warriors of course

Then one of the boys
Had a mishap
Broke off his horse's head

Did you think I would leave you crying
When there's room on my horse for two
Climb up here, Jack
And we'll soon be flying
Up to the sky so blue

And when we grow up we'll always remember
Two little boys in blue

Two little boys
With two little toys
Both grew up tall one day
Both were brave soldiers of course

One boy wore blue
The other wore grey
All on a summer's day

Then one of the boys
Had a mishap
Fell off his horse's back

Did you think I would leave you dying
When there's room on my horse for two
Climb up here Jack and we'll soon be flying
Back to the boys in blue

Cause when we grew up
We always remembered
Two little boys in blue

A CHRISTMAS ROSE

Billy's dead and gone to glory
So is Billy's sister Nell
There's a story I know about them
If I were a poet I would tell

Soft it came as perfumed lavender
Like a breath of country air
Wafted down the filthy alleys
To the barracks, bleak and bare

She was eight this little maiden
And her life had all been spent
In the barracks and the alleys
Where they starved to pay the rent

But she knew enough to tell
To tell this dying boy
You are dying Little Billy
Though in life you've had no joy

Yes I know said little Billy
Ah but sister I don't mind
Gentle Jesus will not hurt me
He's not cruel or unkind

But I can't help thinking sister
That I'd like to take away
Something that you gave me
That I could look at every day

Do you remember in the summer
When the mission took us out
To the green fields and the meadows
Where we ran and played about

Where we ran and played about
With horses there all day
Where no beetles or policeman
Ever frightened us away

Not a word said little Nellie
But at night when Billy slept
On she flung her scanty garments
And down the stairs she crept

Running on and on and on
Nimble as a fawn
Till the day had turned to dawn

When she reached that famous meadow
It was wrapped up in the snow
And Nellie went to Billy
With a rose clasped in her hand

Songs and Poems told by Thelma Agan Paulding

THE BRAVE ENGINEER

T'was a dark stormy night
Not a star was in sight
And a cold north wind was howling down the line

With his sweetheart so dear
Stood a brave engineer
With his orders to ride old number nine

And he kissed her goodbye
With a tear in his eye
For he knew this would be his final ride

As he rounded the hill
His brave heart stood still
For a headlight was shining in his eyes

In the wreck he was found
Lying there on the ground
And he asked them to raise his weary head

As his breath slowly went
This message he sent
To the maiden who thought she would be wed

There's a little white home
That I built for our own
Where I dreamed we'd be happy by and by

Now I leave it to you
Cause I know you'll be true
Till we meet in that golden by and by

BIRMINGHAM JAIL

Write me a letter
Send it by mail
Send it in care of
The Birmingham jail

Roses love sunshine
Violets love dew
Angels in heaven
Know I love you

Know I love you dear
Know I love you
Angels in heaven
Know I love you

Down in the valley
Valley so low
Hang your head over
Hear the wind blow

Hear the wind blow love
Hear the wind blow
Down in the valley
The valley so low

Write me a letter
Send it by mail
Send it in care of
The Birmingham Jail

WINGS OF AN ANGEL

If I had the wings of an angel
Over these prison walls I would fly
Straight to the arms of my darling
And there I would stay till I die

LITTLE ELF MAN

I met a little elf man once
Down where the lilies grow
I asked him why he was so small
And why he did not grow

He raised his head and with his eye
He looked me through and through
"I'm quite as big for me," said he
"As you are big for you."

LITTLE LEM FITCH

At Littleton station
Lived little Lem Fitch
Who tended the station
And minded the switch

Then there's a lot about his baby getting on the train tracks and the train is coming down the
tracks and he can't get there in time to save him.

Then tenderly plying
Each plump little hand
The baby crawled off and rolled down in the sand

God's hand saved my baby
Said little Lem Fitch
Who minded the station
And tended the switch.

THE FRIENDLY COW

The friendly cow
All brown and white
I love with all my heart

She gives me lots of milk to drink
And cream for apple tarts

OTHER POEMS AND STORIES THAT ARE STILL IN PRINT

Winken and Blinken and Nod

The Village Blacksmith

The Gingham Dog and the Calico Cat

Raggedy Ann and Andy

ABOUT THE AUTHOR

Barbara Paulding was born in Hamilton, Iowa in "The Little Black House," a coalminer's shack covered in tarpaper.

Her early life was spent in many different small, southern Iowa towns. Whenever she could, she spent time on her relative's farms, loving the peace and freedom of being in the country. When her mother's parents finally realized their dream of having their own land, Barbara's happiest childhood memories revolved around that little hard scrabble farm.

Although her life has taken many twists and turns, Barbara has never lost her love of the land. Throughout her life she has struggled to find some way to live in the country, to live in peace.

Barbara and her husband, Kirk Moody, live on a small acreage in southern Iowa. She has written a novel, *Ghost Town Truck Stop*, and a family anthology, *Stories From My Father*.